Propulsive yet indeterminate is the wondrous and suspenseful sense of these poems. Speaking the multilemma of living in these times where everything seems to be slipping away and at the same time converging in tsunamis of cataclysmic disaster, the poems are intimate and yet abstract, embodied but evanescent: a phenomenological study, perhaps, of our minds in the Anthropocene, scrambling for certainty but embracing our lack thereof. Acquiescent inner rebellion laced with biting humor astutely observes the calamities swirling around the globe. "What if I say I am a perfect violation/of what's expected of me?" These pages that once were skin will be skin again, always singing like the drowned girl's bone in the old ballad, turned into a flute that wails the story of her death. Dazzling word-dances lead us to intuit a way forward in accepting both a pessimism of the intellect and an optimism of language! You go, grrrl!

   Maria Damon

Laurie Price's *These Pages Once Were Skin*

shows an intelligence that is beautiful in the writing of it. She reaches as far as she can grasp, images and thought-images as if tangent to an unmarked center. There is no map. Her inner life observes her sensorium and its own self. She examines uneasiness as if it were a process. And she knows when to cool down her rhetoric. Poems like these are events of learning.

   John Godfrey

A poet of her own dimension and originality—

elegant, philosophical, wise—Laurie Price's perceptions are heroically true to a language in poetry she crafts and adores. She is *with* the words. We ride inside a rippling sense of place (perhaps a veranda) with balanced yet complex feeling, admiring her precision and inspiring self-reliance, a composure in her poems and their "look," not begging any obsession of self. A wonderful visual artist, as well, who works with the intricate tools that field demands, Price has crossed many borders. She knows how to skillfully recognize and organize the beauties and desires of her own existence. Clearly, an "old soul." "What type of sentences did you have in mind" one poem asks. Pleasure, texture, memory, luminosity, construction, light, dream, lace, paper, a broken window, others and intimacy, conversation, skin. "The world in the word in the work is the work." Just what we all need. ".... zero surprising all/ of me, evening, the tree." I love her "salamander heart."

   Anne Waldman

Reading Laurie Price one steps into a vibrant continuum. Inner and outer worlds, animate and inanimate objects, body, language, and landscape glow and flow, careening into each other. Price has an artist's eye for texture, color, and pattern, "I mix the green and blue with another town which is memory./ Fire burns with dreamy intensity." Her poems are scored to a fractal logic where meanings metamorphose and connotations gather and scatter. This work enables us to experience the anarchy of everyday life, both exhilarating and terrifying. "The journey is never on the map/ the journey is never the map," but somewhere else. The journey is the poem. Hop on for the adventure!

    Elaine Equi

Laurie Price is a poet we poets should have been clamoring for these last three decades. Her work operates in the here and now with the tools of up there and way deep. She is a high-grade lyric philosopher, metallic and transcendent. The sound of her verse is barbed wire and angelic wind. If you know her art work you know what mysteries she uncovers in the public disorder, magical crafts, and guerilla graffiti of Mexico. I find those images alchemically refined in her poetry. Her work is like Mina Loy's, a surprise to my word-jaded reading—and hopefully not just mine.

    Andrei Codrescu

THESE PAGES
ONCE WERE SKIN

Laurie Price

SPUYTEN DUYVIL
New York City

ACKNOWLEDGEMENTS:

Ineffable thanks to Mitch Highfill, for his perspicacious focus and assistance with this manuscript and for his poetry and friendship of more than four decades.

Thanks also to the presses and magazines where some of these poems first appeared, sometimes in earlier versions: *Fence, Talisman, Lyric, How2, The Duplications, The World, Hamilton Stone Review, Black Bread, Pantograph Press, Lunar Chandelier Press, The Arts Fuse* and *Unarmed Submission*. Special thanks to Joe Eliot and Anne Noonan of Situations Press, for publishing my chapbook, *The Assets*, which included material from this collection, to Gary Sullivan of Detour Press, for publishing my chapbook, *Under the Sign of the House*, which also included material from this collection and an earlier version of one poem, to *Unarmed Submission* where an earlier version of one poem appeared, to Ivan Arguelles of Pantograph Press, as one poem previously appeared in *Except for Memory* and finally, to Kimberly Lyons of Lunar Chandelier Press, as one poem previously appeared in *Radio at Night*.

Contents

Yes Now

On the last day of the last month of almost yes
now, last year, no one wins. We don't live free or
die by choice, we die by thousands, by
hundred thousands. There's this constant 'we'
we hear about, see, are told of. Of independence
unbridled by anything save a horse is what
I stream in my dreams. Its urgency. I am
a poet addressing scenery. Yes, I have a small, cozy
beautiful nature though radio rain reception
doesn't mean cake and coffee. It spells wet
met with a rip in a shine designed to project
peril, and could be disguised as light like
a friendly ready to begin hello.
Don't get your hopes up says moi.
Once over the asthma of December what
isn't regret dives into something older
than the royal 'we,' the peasantry, you or me.
It translates to a bigger thing that holds January
hostage and so another year begins. Loop like
noose like lasso'd in. This non-dangerous poem
is a warning This is beseechment This is not
prayer I am a born atheist and ethical.
What if I say I am a perfect violation
of what's expected of me? Nexus for
the orphan disconnects that on 2nd look
conceal ganglia and neutrons open to
modification, alterations; change. Put

a word and a 'nother. Words don't always
collide with meaning. They could be soldiers
in a land-based war; a territorial army formed
against offense and defense. And then all
the land's water dries into itself in ever thirsting
spirals. Large mammals stand guard. This is
where it gets narrative. Stories circle and who
knows which inarticulate transparency you know better,
or which one fails to render. It looks like surrender
but wait, dispersal can save the day in this regard. Observe
those slight tilts of head when reveling in discussion,
that pinprick of light beamed through an eyeglass lens,
cast of shadows around the fingers. To identify or inform,
point out or away, drag what's thinkable with it
in a speakable sense. An intelligence.

Blood parallel

Never in the history of calming down
has anyone ever calmed down
by being told to calm down.

Alarms go off every quarter hour
reminding some to pay more
attention to helicopters
since they hover or
sideswipe thought.

Why don't I find out once
and for all what's going on?

Cross-examined, there's
a lot to think. Blood iron
bruise. Metallic alloys.

The mountains' iron dirt
layers copper with purples
and with air this thin
it becomes hard to breathe.

Everything's an emergency.
The world in the word in the work
is the work. The work in the world
is a word.

Wake me with poetry! Letters
trace the lost. Sing to me eyes
closed just ever so slightly
off tune as if you really
mean it.

ON YOUR WAY

If I seemed to sentence myself with
gravity, less vertical than clunkage
and your words failed to reach me
or rather, all the letters akimbo across
the Atlantic and down over the Keys to
not reach me well then metal and wood,
meddle if they could, I'd have to bail.
A memory made too clear, stereo voice,
anticipation parallel with hope,
a pheromone in its own right,
would not exceed your belief. Or mine.
Let's talk about it then, about how a spark
seemed to point to some future moment
when. And then this is when. You are on
your way. This is that day we agreed to
wait for, and we did it, speechless.

WENT

Striking out from the offshore gallery
moon pale behind the earth, conveying
ripeness fully later would be of us, before
lifting elements of logic from the grip
of handsome resolves, which don't fix
anything so much as place us
somewhere unfamiliar. Bonecracking
chainsmoking me went, had, while some
where else one was being as they are.
Turned to fold in what might be thought about.
Might at its least. Cancellation
of landscape. Grey streets. Rain.

CHRYSALIS

A need to charge a slight shiver
to talk through an enthusiasm
off the trail. Yellow catches my breath
and a stand of reflections pitch
together in their own sac.
Showgirl chrysalis bobs up and down
in furious punctuation of slighted extracts.
Winter falls with the sun's descent.
Anathema! yet weary, dissonant tho'
luminous birds call from a center
where things are practical, flocked
within themselves, like a ballet
dancer's voice and thoughts.

ELSEWISE

Approximately meters from chaos
 we drop "near." Come closer.
As usual, the sun or stars
lope across the sky, they do not
whisper another another another
as they pass. One day
I'm talking to you
and then, well, I'm just not.

The stars make fools of you and your obstacles.
Your headaches, the gerrymandered sum of you.

This is the wildness of
human beings – how they
turn ugly, turn away.

Everything formal, white-gloved wave,
tidal wave, that thing you can't purge.

We're all always at
various stages of
waking up,
going to sleep.

The printer gives birth to
a first draft, it's *not* Caesarian, but
if I'm not careful and don't
hold my hands out
to receive the page
it spills to the floor.

At night

Dogs bark, first one,
then maybe three and
pretty soon up and down
the block, from neighbor's rooftops,
dogs of all sizes and timbres argue and
present in full chorus.

When it's night it's always night.
We live for that
relentless metaphysical backdrop.
Hours like trampolines—
there's a metaphor for that
to arrow the search and drive it further in.

Any moment an infinitesimal space
might open above something
broken where something else is broken.
A wreck of motion slipshods the reckless core
which is movement, kinetic and frictive, how
fractals unspool the wholes.

ACROSS THE SKY

the rise and fall of light on objects
yokes a trundle barely seized

birds sound out the drastic sluice
or collide swirled in pull

moving faster now than high wires
battered by systems, more at wind

the journey is never on the map
the journey is never the map

the rules of the game deliver
is a linear correspondence

squalling birds learn a distance flat
is the kind of phrase cultivating

more songs somewhere
by everything you do

ACTION

There's a future speeding towards you.
Supportable. There is exact trust.
There's the inclination to describe
confusing a silver auto at night
with light. Three things clock in
at the divine surface of a color's red.
Matamoros becomes *Murguía*. Undebatable
even as the lights change.

ADDENDUM

Russell you're dead but you're still in my head
and heart, you showed me some different arts
& I already had a few ghosts, you knew.
When I wrote, "dead or alive, my friends
are always with me," we spoke frankly
of our dead, the wave we'd lived through
in SF, losing everyone, and I'd even smoked
the ashes of a close friend mixed with hash.
That you'd survived all that was a comfort
& you were right there above my head,
upstairs. Now you're always with me.

Blessing

cold but not wet and very high up
the work is slow and riddled with revisions
bullets   quiet revolutions   neither velvet
nor contract   somewhat to the north
is a sound falling   its reveal codes   activated

in the hills, called *cerro*   pitched between
the manufactured sense of a weather forming
red and white towers   splintery surge of green
leaves lit by clouds w/possibly religious overtones
gold and white god rays   pigment the air   filtering

The yesterday sentence
looks perfect now, thank you.

Love is easy to patch so that
its color makes you amble against
saggy anticipations harsh with heat.
Steam clarifies that stretch.
Being armed with concrete
where a patina features auto exhaust black
against a mustard back
drop near a door.
Door could open. I order
a chicken korma. The authorities are asleep or
dumb or acting dumb and those
they appeal to dumbfound me.
Virtual environments have their own hierarchy.
Almonds exist crushed with butter and cream.
Gauze is a sash there is no mirth.
How does measure target a tense end?
How does damage allocate a middle?
He says he wants me because I make him
feel happy and he will cook for me.
When I want to engage I open
a new window.

PRECISELY AT THE EDGE OF WHAT WE WANT

to call history is something
exhaustedly imposed as natural order.
I wanted to keep these things
secret as anyone does.
Was I thinking of you?
In the I'm not here you are here continuum
lurk danger zones. No equivocation
makes it possible to distort the link.
Because you get lost in the book of loss
is personal. Specific awareness of the spaces
left empty is not enough to rid you
of your need to believe in something formal
though others have mastered this
with disappointing results.
The day with its weary heat
seems impossible no relief or rain
even small wind to blow the burning
from this valley. The book of loss
is no help here. I found that the pages
turning was a dog barking
where I'd encountered someone Dear.
You might call that coincidence
not to guide us
but that we insist on concretions
in a word.

BEAUTY

ductlike or ductive
in whose understanding
we are alone, connectivity
being an arbitrary discovery
Diphthong   Deep throat   Kaleidoscoping
and what that gives – or obscures totals one two three
four *khamsa*. The hand. It resist. Or hold

The hold
        is preface enough

Warm details in a
humid atmosphere
Something round about
to spiral a question away
from its circumvention
and how that gives
value or contains
phrases often trilled in
language marvels
beached like marbles

Hollow buildings fragment
deceased on city corners,
strands brick and brack,
wails of stray cats

You and I agree there's
a tree and it's vertical
After that, things get
        nervous

UNCLEAT

for Rebecca Loudon

Rebecca the dogs are dead
shrimp heads scrape against
my marble-floored tomb
Artichoke blood leaks green
and mars a dish
and fish, this pungenty
this   an urgency   this dead this
scent of curriculum

The crystals of my vertigo
dislodge from yr atmosphere
You've got one circular waterway
that bring fish back to spawn

I love a thin blue light
The laughter of the unemployed
keeps me awake at night until dawn
Somewhere else it's raining or

tide bursts high or fingers slide
into gloves and there's a store
that stays open all night where neon
blinks red and blue

I lose the patrician –
go ahead, unsnap the Spencerian
odes and watch the wings
of your dark dictionaries
uncleat

LODE

When every person is
a credible force yet by
each beautiful ruin this
degree of ideals gates
the imagination,
remote contemplations yield
inspiration's service as
a voice in a temple might
cavern and gating greed
freed from ego cede
a new joy: tender heart.

THE HARD WAY

Just details at best and slow to recover
according to the continues. Midwinter light
brands the ridiculous sublime and a quartet
eking out My Way does me in. We're flushing
the human toilet, putting silly stipulations on that
which should take preference: a rounded triage
of maxims akin to toe to heel, top to bottom
just complicates further by the aim to beguile.
Yet there is a haunted one, a hunted one
and a brave one within the maze of what's virtuous.
Who is served blows the lid off centuries' inquests
and pursuits. The natural order beset by cheap frauds
so continuous their circles hide any truths. It's the rain
now lightly sewing and bobbing through the drains.
You do the hokey pokey and you turn yourself around.
That's what it's all about.

DEVICES

I am a round
shadow receptor
a purveyor of scrap
hanger of lines.

Hookers walk in
walkers hooked in
to devices ear eye
throat nosey don't
exist time to kiss
and make up in
defense of at times.

Our blue ocean event is annihilative
and no kidding it's ours and what it is.
The rest is drag and spill.
Can I draw you there?

Text dictates into being
thought intuits and
conscious effort to hold
against the background
noise
within which
tea mint rain
doesn't fall
away for sun
as grey grows
casual in that
faithful door
swung
shut behind me.

SKEWERED WITH DIS-EASE I MADE NOTES

for the poem instead of actually
writing it. There was too much
to say and I needed time.
Not nostalgia. Not piano
chords descending a scale
like nudes descending
a staircase to end up in never
arrive. An old man picks up and
carries his old dog across the street.
Any moment one of us could
falter, fall, fail. We are so frail.

Rain

I fix the light forward in a temperature of continuing.
Water verticals drip grey with grey lines and chiaroscuro'd
jolt the memory stagger to dispatch – this time from the obvious
squeeze of faking silence by distracting sounds from their echoes.
This suddenly ends and is nowhere. In particular. While mind's
this glimpse of process becomes a gem, rain falls metallic
and diagonal through narrow shafts of cold air and day. Time
coincides, is coincident. Man with plastic bag for a hat dashes
past a running nun. No one's got an umbrella; no way to cover.

HALFTIME

Right away you think you know
what you've exhausted.
A light snaps on in the kitchen
the vertical surfaces glaze. And each of
the half-inch parameters you'd identified
dissolve with it. The boys ply their
domino effect, a larger manufacture than
any solo effort brings. There are three
movements that evolve into a final clap
& curtains again when someone says
"2 tickets" . . . "a lovely program."
The origin of chattel is clothbound, half signatures.
Even in a restive state you feel the temptation.
Something starts up again, some blank disclaimer.

August 4th 2017

Somewhere else in the valley it's pouring
& thunder rolls toward, past, moves over
closer, stretches out, extends. The same core
hides or reveals sound and viscous grey clouds.
Cat quickly sips water & drain makes a backed-up swish.
I wish inside of it. I stroke the cat, who's made
an S alongside me with her tail wound
around my arm. Now she turns and sighs, closes
her eyes as I rub her belly. Aladdin never had it
so good. I'm here with her; she's here with me.
Secrets and mysteries expose and conceal.
Wind lifts light curtains, another whoosh. I wish
every day were like this; words smooth as fur
and quiet before a proverbial storm hits. Time
to sit and contemplate a day unlike my others.
Flowers, named dahlias, I never thought I could love
based on their name, but they came from a woman
who said she'd carried them down from the mountains
to town, heavy fuchsia puffs, radiant and
lush in her arms, now on my table in a vase.

Remote

A cologne named Siesta or
a bus route dubbed Beethoven
misplace the detachment of
solo distances from the getgo.
When I hit this green button
there you are a field of mirrors.
I reference the discontinuities:
To write and engage by love
& money desires impulse,
concentrated persistence
sometimes though not
altogether, almost
that.

Forget It

When inflection bleeds from
eyebrows arched and arrowed
toward a hook-like pout.
When a put-in gawk
cleaved to angers & doubt
draws endlessly down:
Fuck you and your frown.

MILAGRO

If with care towards promise
I break my silent vow
to enter, opened
as no other place will allow.
There oughta be a name for this.
Okay I'm going to sit very still now
watch October squeeze the light
to a thin line. My friends
are always with me
dead or alive and music changes things
or my hands too are not the same. Here
there's a green glass
with a clear stem
and you in green leaf
of pressed maple. October
is written on the sky
seen from a rock. All the hard things
are here to stay. Durable, this duration
of unbuttoning the blushes
invents a shift in color. Everything
here plus you.

COVER

I sacrificed my land for your thoughtful gesture.
Plum wind, stinging fresh behind a thick curtain
clouded that picture. The one I drew you
with my hand. Another gesture as if to say
it in a list lost among subjects, verbs, nouns.
I had the notion that to set it free would put
me right. Only then could I glance the peripheral,
admittedly fractal stretches. What could wrest
me from the next chapter. The 'tis of thee.

No rest

here truly here the turbulent touch
of you is precise

pieces of remember stuck
into what we've skilled

or I have and hope for the best
no poison harpoon

where a heart is
was between us

since it is always the rest
between us

gives no rest

As Much Through or Not

We were always one another, yes,
and trust was art as much as art
was trust. Our journey: a series
of unconscious arcs between here and
there that bonded us. Small doses doled
seven different ways could make a week.
Always close, sometimes closer, as much
through our stuff as odd one out in how
our feet threaded together or not.
This is the story of a younger us.
A fictional us. Admiration, in effect.
An us that could ride hit or miss in
either your head or mine. An us that
polished the essences of each –
grounded in the marvelous.

As dream might

Too bright for walking when the waking's hot
clunky mass release paraphrases
the dull thud forward and scrapes as always.

The too hot fits to these seizures –
little round things in things
like sun moves smaller back –
arrange to no collusion.

Time to graft these punctuations
in dull thud places then
off the surface of glass.

Deep pitches catalog on a helix
what carries from a body
grant as might what could live
and spoken there rest easily understood.

This shrill again closes the imaginary cleft
used to join all the snippets of light
seized from somewhere
in the wake of that imagining
begets the sky letterwriting
bluer than body cold
to read into
and fall back
as dream might.

Winds Blow

these words and ornaments
also the principles from
an articulate kindness
that wait for a long time
under some trees, addressing
the parts leading what we know
into the room

IN ITS BECOMING

The room settles into its deepest sense
from the bottom up layered and fades
fast in its becoming
as though its properties were sinking
enough to say its geology being of interest
would hide its absolute thingness of concrete and glass
felt no differently then than window through
and pictured in its frame a tree that parallels
the shape of its becoming

Trees in the shapes of trees
"collecting toward the greenest cone"
wait to be seen as such
stall against time and portraiture
split hastily to cradle
how our corner of the world
might come to continue
enchanting

ROOM WITH A VIEW

Things to charm and entrance you alarm
and beg forgiveness. Water by the hour
knocks out all the figures. Body count
impressionable, not lacking in charm.
Sing to it how night falls wanting to be
a window you could see through.

Black Hawthorne

Only to tremble that I am a bird
I remain my own fear
                              Breathe
in a nest today walking more softly
Pink-white eggs concealed
                                        Daydreaming
only pictures
                        traces nothing found
under the sign of the house
likely to attract

To concede the house since nesting
                                        Feel calmer
stretches of absolute space
Two branches as shelter
                        pure sound of a patient sky
would-be glow
                                    of an underworld
besieged by cognizance
Trembled as poles

And Shifting

A little Scarlatti and the earlier blue
above, some heaven not bursting
open settles in cold light painting bricks
and shifting starts the new year
about a new lease weightlessness
no content achieves. History running
in place self-referential and continuous
could be included was a don't
but understands itself now. Not scrambling
to outdo the inevitable from solidifying
threatens to muck up the works
but the sameness is more of the same.
Tree shadows lick the sidewalk
two girls walking and never breach
the open window the gravitational urge.
Air. There is nothing that sticks less.
It simply and what lights there.

RECIPROCALS

The courtyard below the balcony is comforting
Or simply corresponds to what's irresistible
Sequences of windows arranged in perfect squares
Paint gridded moonlight on the tiles

The line of no hints stutters in the gleam
And the visible interior couched nearby
Some phantom as if glass
Calling light were smoke

We forget our devotions
Spare graces hushing the sky
Fingers turreted in lunar spill
Stored words idling

LISTEN

Broken through the glare of hedgelights
fed out along a highway like gigantic trees
are real trees, noted, braided
in among simian shadows.
An itchy arc defines
something precise, assimilated
the way one arrives at conclusions
believing them as if they were more than.

NUMBERS

They said I was to be this doll this girl
this house this twig the falling windows
would open on a false thing and I too
could be perplexed. Someone about whom
we wouldn't notice and suffered ordeals
at the hand of re-entry. I suppose was all
I could say the relaxing argument rolled
to a fist. Come Spring sleep's butterflies
were slow to come and fewer of them.
The noon of them and their verbs crashing
like nouns and nighttime appointed delights.
All the instruments of zero surprising all
of me, evening, the tree.

No other reason

for S.E., rip

At that point I should've known
the transparent distances shouldering
wanted to tempt me to betray
my path was useful and had relation
which has no wrongful end
to accommodating the work
that then flowered. To enter is not exact.
No leaving has less place
or where nothing has been joined
there scattering. To dream the path
that doesn't narrow or possess one
to the other even with reason.
Enough for all that can. What can
hold the sense of the same thing.
A way of hearing more and keeping.
No other reason.

One way to put it

Time winters in a forest fall of black
conclusions. We shake what lists
from the hush. We shake the trees.
Into that clearing comes a basic intelligence.
I show you my pen, my sword, my that.
That a reason for things could exist
in such clutter. Winds blow some leaves
from the trees. Words chase their meanings.

A Broad Arc

for James Ruggia

I am speaking or singing and it won't monetize.
There was a time. And then there were other times.
All this before BYOD (bring your own device) intervened,
interfered, matriculated my thoughts (which do not monetize).
A plane flew so low overhead this morning I thought
it would crash into a tree or church dome but it swept
a broad arc around the valley before gaining altitude.
Thinking can be like that. A broad arc and altitude.
It too doesn't monetize. Smiles of hostile ones
conjure zeroes while the smiles of hospitable ones
confer impressions. Dreaming cheshire you, cherish
the view from a storey with a story, its altitude.
Protagonists crowd around a lamp post but tonight
a bronze moon draws close to a tree, hangs off its
lowest branch. I'd like to think this means something.
Squeeze it tight. Wring the rings those protagonists
run below. Who are you? You're a little bit late you've
just arrived and it's clear I'll accept any theory as excuse.
And then an angel's blue opium eyes unclose.

Before I'm done

November passed fast. The glasses frames ordered and sent broke almost immediately upon receipt. Now I sit and watch black gulls and salmon-colored clouds move across white clouds and a blurry 2/3 moon at the beach. Can you distinguish between a fall sky and a winter sky? Do gulls go somewhere? How do they know it's time? It's warm here so I guess they stay and swoop and circle in pirouettes above the water while pelicans dive straight down for their prey. We humans always hesitate, leave things for last. I've been letting everyone I love know I love them, now, before I'm done or they're done. Some folks get it and some folks just don't. There's always at least one.

I NEVER DECIDED IT

so many things
drifted towards it
the digital contexts, content
midnight – four zeroes
divided by a colon
four *ojos* divided
by a nose

Butoh

Willful doesn't plead or remonstrate
connecting teapots to rock gardens.
Floating reeds face a bare cliff wall.
What that means could be demonstrable:
a thin expanse of water. On days like this
we might levitate to heaven with
our muted demands by all accounts
in the realm of possible thinking
impossible to shake, domain
of the possible – thoughts not
yet shook.

We Want Your Shoe

We want an adjustable sadness to cover for meaninglessness. We want to walk and drink coffee from a cardboard cup. We want your spies. We want brunch. The scent of your smile pains me, the royal we.

The keyboard begets the keyboard's smoke and mirrors dance. This night is almost young and I feel yes. I track its smell. I smell a rat. Magnetic forces gummy shit does not fly.

She said *me cago en dios*. I shit on god. I want a bottom line that's not desperation. This vulgar night sentinel. Its passing traffics.

TRAFFIC

Paralyzed in paradise
self existing sacredness
of world a luminous allegory
in white lilies and crystal.
Categorical questions indict.
Can hope and hell co-exist?
My power steering away from
you's no good. Taxi indifference
launches yellow blur at just
the velocity I want. City smells
burnt and oily as grey increase
overtakes the visor and casual
like the visitor I am
not paying any mind.

SMOKING AGAIN

He could just drive her out, run for cover
run his points for going down
to the nowhere else, his garden living
in him like him in his flat. A road was what he said.
Excessive not to trust the landscape to enter
the ruin of his shirt, him, and smoking again.
The center of his breath loved him, watched him
alone like that, push it front and center.

Going In and Out

Saturday's dusty syllables stir
a waking fold that's intricate,
etched with sudden shapes
thieved and flung backwards and sky
reminds me that no place is eternal;
rope perforates and shreds, threads
sponge the ink in my head
to spread a rumor, dart in a dark circle
that surrenders night to us, going
in and out, in and out, like stars breathe
and now your hand spreads air flat
'round us, describes what you and
no one else wants to see, who don't
see their part in any thing, they just part
the air. Here. Like there's a line to link
all the threads from Friday and press
them back to before they began.

HAVING NOT SAID ENOUGH

The daily chase running circles
'round the clock stand still
again to fall dry

Smiles from the dying
passages, edged or formed
before the end of the line
interrupts the occasion

Nothing, but less grows
if failed thus

Paled conclusions reached
by boat again a gradual
rendering of way through
to purpose the stillness
you could thread through

Stream running thin
and underground

LETTERS

like poems, a hush of sky
blue flutters through
the air urgently undoing
the distance of their absence
before restlessly continuing
upon arrival, the way
telling continues, is
continuous

Smear

The street at night, bottle built to what makes
you feel the citizens lust for cover. Crazy hair
do sneaks up from behind a stranger's hand
lifts a pink cloud dancing over Chapultepec
where the wide angle gives a bit.
Black holes slant and ill wind coughs
plastic grit. The city, acrid in its mess.
I struggle to want it to fade
its filthy stain positions.

OF YOUR PASSING

for Larry Fagin

To confront my allergy to suffering
you talk'd risk and persistence. Open
you said I couldn't be torn apart.

Yes, paragraphs might be
allowed, even encouraged.
My innumerable rehearsals
were amiably social,
boisterous I thought
they'd never end after all.

On your home soil I witnessed
the book police as more likely to
scorn intellect than some hip postures.

It's all medication and medicated,
drones we see "them" as, drones
"they're" partial to, drones that
fall in love with other drones.
This "relationship," this white
boy high-five silencing some "us" –
orchestrates narratives
that disarm me and you and
I meet some parts you like,
suffer their perfect effects,
use what's there to properly see
themselves or me free of "them" – or you –
and this tinge really hurts, really
captures that dosed imagination.

After Easter, before Ramadan began,
the blog trunk burst with news
of your passing. My allergy, by the way
has no cause; it's strictly mental.

But here's the rub: to be impressed
by time or informed ink, embittered
by books or jobs, is to be bereft of
the benefits of this mixture of morning
with elegance and light with caffeine.

Ascendant ciphers create benevolence –
gestures slaked to thirst
engage to work harder,
be braver; check the intentions
at each approach.

And you, you too.
After detonating so much ire
and enmity; at the end, it's love,
no? That push.

Paradox of Two

With language and the body, breath
is breadth. Culture was existence,
elevated, diastolic, included oral & esoteric trials
chronologically important to understand
to maintain recognition apart from narrative.

I mean the problem of how to be free
is epistemological, and the power needed
to be true to both sides of one's brain
escapes inquiry. The essential paradox
of two begets life and death, amplified.
But there's no narrative; it's a fragile
fucked up mess and we just accommodate.

In space, poetry is a circumstantial essence.
Who doesn't know the view? Any decorated
presentation is a lie lit by some white blotch
called the sun. It's not religious nor is it
abstract. There are trees that mirror concepts
of identity, not so much mystical as unconscious.

POEMS syndrome*

Sky striates in shades of salmon and earth pink
while tin roof percusses under sun shower –

Neighbors blast romantic Mexican tunes
across the hollow which intensify with the sky's
deepening. Coffee is good and strong, everything
I couldn't feel since before yesterday.

Music inside is shrill in that avant garde way where
a violin shows off its modulations and tones, makes
a moment last an hour. It's the computer radio, not
my mind-ear. Is it good or just a space filler?

I review this question and inspect lines
on a page. My cat sleeps because my bed is
sumptuously comfortable and this weather
begs her to stay put. I was there until
I popped awake with a sudden desire
for coffee and to work, but I can't
bear it. I can't bear how askew
my synapses are this morning.

The nervous system signs in its own language.
Thrum of vitriol and vitality clock in at rounds.
Temperature responds to ambition, waxes
warm when elocution bears empathy – goes
silent when the mind (and therefore all other parts)
is incapable of integration. The stuck out
sticking out thing begs attention.

POEMS syndrome occurs 1.5 times more frequently
among men than women; the typical age of POEMS
syndrome onset is adults in their 50s and the disorder
is chronic. Helter skelter thoughts ramble at will.

Poets are particularly susceptible to contracting it
of course and can, also at will, pass it to others –
think of an exquisite corpse, each section
unknown to the next recipient
hidden in folded secret.

You might have a fever, the fever might rise to such
a high temperature that it shreds the immune system –
darkens and thickens the skin, eliminates diffidence,
                        produces excessive hair growth. Male pattern baldness
and lack of ambition are things of the past. Or so it
might seem. Some reactions are static. How to move
forward with no desire to do so? I am generally *not*
susceptible to such meanderings but I display
or express a reluctance to display or express.

Swope rhymes with hope but the resemblance ends there.
Swope is a person who loves haters. Swope is when
you are the shit and you know it and don't give a fuck.
It's when all you do is win. Swope – so outside my scope.

POEMS syndrome doesn't bring relief or clever phrases.
The head doesn't swell yet the neck becomes a stump
where individual words can be stacked while they wait
consideration. There is no issue that won't benefit
from empathy. Em. Greek for 'in'. Path, sometimes strewn
with rose petals, mostly not. Y is 'and' in Spanish. Empathy.

Sometimes what's hard to know is
what's esoterically buried or hidden or
maybe a synapse that's lodged cold
starts to singe its own edges not unlike
paper magnet sun but for the hundredth
time there's no time like the present; no
time at all equivalent to what's been frozen.

Or a feeling begets a wish to know more, to
investigate but not interrogate the preceding
impulse that came from "nowhere" like "nothing."

A vector, I submit to some territorial pull forward –
an inclination or inkling that does not present itself
but suddenly, vertiginously, the world begins to spin
and stays within the range of low thrum for weeks.

Centrifugal cogency intervenes. I walk through a bramble
of roots and vines towards a water source. The air ribbons
through this stuff and carries earth; dust. Insect wings
fall away on the breeze. I have everything I need.

*https://www.mayoclinic.org/diseases-conditions/poems-syndrome/symp-
toms-causes/syc-20352678   POEMS syndrome is a rare blood disorder
that damages your nerves and affects other parts of your body. POEMS stands for
these signs and symptoms: **Polyneuropathy.** Numbness, tingling and weakness
in your legs — and over time, maybe in your hands — and difficulty breathing.
This is an essential feature in the diagnosis of POEMS syndrome. **Organomegaly.**
Enlarged spleen, liver or lymph nodes. **Endocrinopathy/edema.** Abnormal hor-
mone levels that can result in an underactive thyroid (hypothyroidism), diabetes,
sexual problems, fatigue, swelling in your limbs, and problems with metabolism
and other essential functions. **Monoclonal-protein.** Abnormal bone marrow cells
(plasma cells) that produce a protein (monoclonal protein) that can be found in
the bloodstream. This is an essential feature in the diagnosis of POEMS syndrome.
Monoclonal-protein is often associated with unusual bone hardening or thick-
ening. **Skin changes.** More color than normal on your skin, red spots, possibly
thicker skin, and increased facial or leg hair.

Noose and some glue

Laurie Price

NOOSE AND SOME GLUE

What is this rope that breaks
the surface   carves a curve

ties wire and white paper
to braided rope and some glue
yet looks like gypsum?

That white of shapes falling falling
falling away to words, what – is
the description wrong
exploded from its composition,
does that matter?

Troubles graphic as noose
weave together and shadow
where they tear so that sewn
it's like a raiment.

In the impression which is dark
though gypsum white noose cum
rope hangs ready but is benign,
beyond comfort but benign.

Walk around these things
where a lasso binds thoughts
that needle and thread links seam.

This texture that shapes evocations,
shape that intimates your irrational fears
glued to assumption –
There can be
no light lit
in that darkness.

El dogal
y algo de pegamento

Laurie Price

El dogal y algo de pegamento

Que es esta cuerda que se rompe
la superficie   talla a una curva

que ata alambre y papel blanco
a la cuerda trenzada y un poco de pegamento
mientras aparece aljez?

Ese blanco de formas cayendo
cayendo en palabras, ¿qué? –
es la descripción incorrecta
estallado de su composición,
¿eso importa?

Molestias tan gráficas como el dogal
tejer juntos y poner una sombra
donde se rompen así que cuando cosido
es como una vestidura.

Dentro la impresión que es oscuro
aunque el aljez blanco, dogal, soga especie
cuerda, cuelga listo pero es benigno,
más allá de la comodidad pero benigno.

Caminar alrededor de estas cosas
donde un lazo ata los pensamientos
que pinchan y los enlaces de hilo en unión.

Esta textura que moldea a las evocaciones
forma que insinúa tus miedos irracionales
pegado a la suposición –
Puede haber
no luz encendida
en esa oscuridad.

Geometry

Perpendiculars

I brought these words together
to see how they'd say.
They locate against luxury, curious to speech.
An ear hears queer melody.

With the rain came the first inching toward desire.
What would you like, something silver? There are no routes
to follow, no getting to. Some days only this lace curtain
surprises the window. A piece of paper, some inkling or idea.
Clouds stretch thin to cover a glutinous moon,
pull into milky pockets as they move in a mass.
Telephone sings high F, impatient repetition
of the same note sustains when there could be silence.

Fuchsia rhododendron petal spins askew to the floor.
Pink with temerity, shoulders no longer encased
but balancing and demure. Persistence built by pauses,
shows strength.

I think about everything which takes a long time.
The mirror serves as surface, only surface.
Identification has laws of trust.
Something noble, but empty. Individual truths.

Storm clouds gradually tear. Finally a hint of place
above always there, now part of this picture.
Mountains are slow. We collect, we walk, shovelful
by shovelful. Bits of broken glass bring back the sun.
This was a valley. Now it's a hill.

In another town it is always later. I used to wonder
if a place ever caught up with another. When you walk
do you feel divisions of time pass from minutes to molecules?
This was a great worry though I never lost sleep.

I dreamed a circle of web-like threads that kept
all animate presences in place for almost my full
first ten years. Sometimes the web was my hand
and I felt threads pull my fingers into alpha-
betical gestures. A droning sound accompanied
by singing voices controlled the atmosphere
and intensity of movement.

More colors and shapes collide than I have time for now.
Extract the symbols and paste them to your heart
so I can stop making suggestions.

        Is this the perfect moment?

Descriptions could be short like meadow, forest, water, fire,
                or with more clarity more rain and an angry ocean
                rebuilds the coast. From the road:
                sand blooms in suspension off the beach;
                greenish foam of dead fish.

I mix the green and blue with another town which is memory.
Fire burns with dreamy intensity.
Misunderstanding clothes this landscape.
Quick pull the thread from the needle.
Stream runs thin
and underground.

CONSTRUCTION

What type of sentences did you have in mind?
All of beauty arrives in pleasure.
                    All that passes is time, is memory.
Vowels hang low off the tongue.
The harsh range this light makes
seeps in patches under the skin.
This dream appears too early
in cold winter greens,
figures of speech.
                    Light tumbles down the back stair
(forming the foreground)
on doors closed, a broken window.
A certain august one sits on the veranda
of a tiny club.
                    It is always night and always a city.
In the hot stillness of this roadstead steam is clearly audible.
Garden shadows foliate the lawn.
Pleated light is glaringly obvious.
Transparent forest sweeps up the center
but all too often, beauty
as a mask for much that is deadly
forms no exception;
the continuous treatment by amateurs
too serious to be moved.

CIRCLES

The odds of persuasion indicate
a definite location in space.
The one evidence: the face.
A likeable sentence.

Dispelled of narrative
words are empty frames: blue
surrounds night, filters light.
When cars pass it sounds like rain

soft through windows clear as glass
but heavy like curtains. Salamander
heart swims against wall. This heart
of mine, how it shines below
dirt below sand below hills.

The Distance

Shadows of hidden words cause us to turn our heads,
rustle with busyness to lose the shadows.
Clouds float across the clearest sky.
We mistake the clouds for shadows, though
the clouds are empty, swirls of gaseous white.
Shadows dictate the speed of ground,
of distance covered, yet what is
before us is visible:

Heat lifts in waves from dangerously hot sidewalks
and still I move my feet, one after the other
conscious of the difficult air.
Your absence forms a hole I pass through
again and again. The possible variations.
The impossible redress. Some words said
and a black X followed by more clouds.
My body below this column of air.
And you there.

POINTS OF DEPARTURE

In a more abstract world
language works to indifference;
the music assigns a code of agreement.
I see your hands, your face.
This breath is mine forever
and there's more.

Under the spell of November
a delicate hour precedes sleep.
Touch that loosens
these priorities gripped at the seams
sings gentle and wan.
Whatever loses, it's by touch, by feel.

Walk and sleep with your own particulars.
Let the hands know each trick.
If home were someplace to be I would go there
but the rooms have bled thin.
For all the days' sleep there is none.
Breaking weather clouds,

condition of air folds and turns
promises back from priority.
I walk this walk,
sing this song,
do this thing
till it's done.

LINES AND SEGMENTS

Sensation begins when I place my hand
upon my heart and feel the warmth
of other bodies. I hold this now
and carry it with me but
it is never the same.

Time is animal hide
turning pages that once were skin.
All the secrets of your life
were here before you.
The predator instinct is still intact.
Each bruise attests to that.

LAURIE PRICE is a poet and visual artist who was in the first graduating class at Naropa's (then Institute) Jack Kerouac School of Disembodied Poetics in 1981 and has since published poetry and made and exhibited her visual art (laurie-price.com). Courtesy of a generous year-long Gerbode Foundation Poetry grant received in 1993 she moved to Oaxaca, Mexico to begin her life as a citizen of the world. Since then she's lived in Morocco, Spain, and now resides in Oaxaca, Mexico (since 2013). Two full-length collections (Except for Memory [Pantograph Press, Berkeley, CA, 1993] and Radio at Night: Recent and Selected Work [Lunar Chandelier Press, 2013] and four chapbooks have been published. Her work has appeared in Talisman, Eoagh, HOW2, Big Allis, Arshile, The East Village and Fence, among other magazines. A new ms., entitled Pages That Once Were Skin is in the works and you can view her photos & artworks here:

http://graciouseconomiesandcorrugatedshadows.blogspot.com (2009-2022)
and here:
https://graciouseconomiesandetc2.blogspot.com/
(current).

www.ingramcontent.com/pod-product-compliance
Lightning Source LLC
Chambersburg PA
CBHW031250120626
46545CB00007B/2741